Messages & Reminders FROM D.p. Divine parent

VOLUME I

by Dr. Sherrilyn Kirchner

Balboa Press books may be ordered through booksellers or by contacting:

Balboa Press
A Division of Hay House
1663 Liberty Drive
Bloomington, IN 47403
www.balboapress.com
844-682-1282

Because of the dynamic nature of the Internet, any web addresses or links contained in this book may have changed since publication and may no longer be valid. The views expressed in this work are solely those of the author and do not necessarily reflect the views of the publisher, and the publisher hereby disclaims any responsibility for them.

Any people depicted in stock imagery provided by Storyblocks are models, and such images are being used for illustrative purposes only. Storyblocks.com

ISBN: 979-8-7652-3707-6 (sc)
ISBN: 979-8-76523-709-0 (hc)
ISBN: 979-8-7652-3708-3 (e)

Library of Congress Control Number: 2022922488

Print information available on the last page.

Balboa Press rev. date: 12/31/2022

Dedicated to all Divine children.

— CONTENTS —

— A MESSAGE FROM DR. K. —

Welcome, Divine child. I am Dr. Sherrilyn Kirchner, a metaphysician specializing in holistic healing. In working with my clients over the years, I've noticed a common need for a completely supportive and all-accepting parental figure that can offer beneficial advice, undivided attention, complete acceptance, and unconditional love. To fill that need, I created *D.p.* (Divine parent).

D.p. is an icon that represents the ideal parental figure. The parent who supports without judgment, who loves without condition, and who guides without doubt. The most important thing to remember about D.p. is that this parent lives within you. You are never separated from D.p. — D.p. is always with you. D.p. is a part of you.

This is the first volume in a series of *Messages & Reminders from D.p.* for anyone who wishes to understand, embrace, and hone their Divine creative power.

Live in the Body, Master the Mind, Witness through Spirit.

— Dr. K.

NOTE: Please refer to the Glossary at the end of this book to further familiarize yourself with the key concepts used throughout this series.

— INTRODUCTION —

Greetings, Divine child. I am *D.p.*, your Divine parent. I reside within the eternal Divine consciousness, which resides within you.

My ultimate purpose is to help awaken in you a renewed awareness of the immense power that lives within you by offering *Messages & Reminders* of forgotten truths. Deep down, you know of your powerful creation abilities, but because of the veil of the human experience, most of you have forgotten your true creative potential. In order to create the life you want, it is vitally important that you remember these truths and implement them into your life.

As Divine children, you have a Divine right to experience all that you desire. You are already using your Divine creative power by attracting and allowing this book into your life. Now is the time to delve further and connect to your immense power within. In this endeavor, I offer you unconditional love, support, and acceptance.

D.p.

— HOW TO BENEFIT FROM THESE MESSAGES & REMINDERS —

This book is designed to provide insight on certain self-empowering principles along with weekly practices to help you implement each principle into your daily life. The Messages and Reminders are organized in a progressive fashion, but if you feel called to work out of order, please follow your intuition. See what resonates with you. Regardless of how you progress through the book, know that there is no right or wrong way. Just remember that implementation is key. It's easy to understand a concept. It's much more challenging — and rewarding — to implement these concepts into your daily life.

The weekly practices encourage focus and effort. I suggest you choose a certain day of the week on which to explore each week's Message or Reminder. It may help to add a daily reminder on your calendar to keep track of which Message or Reminder you're focusing on that week, in addition to utilizing the notes section to track your experience. Ultimately, you are in charge of your life, and you decide how you want to approach and interact with this information.

I recommend you set your intentions each day and listen for your truths to emerge. *What do you want to get out of this? What changes do you want to create?* Keep a record. Write out your intentions and your newfound awareness along with any challenges and successes. It will be much easier to see your progress that way.

Remember, this work is up to you. No one else can evolve for you. You already have everything you need within you. All you have to do is make the choice to continue. Complete self-love is the key to unlock any door, and you hold this key within.

Messages & Reminders

FROM

D.p.

ABOUT MY...

Self

I am D.p.

D.P. STANDS FOR
DIVINE PARENT.

I AM AN ICON
THAT IS HERE
TO HELP YOU
REMEMBER WHO
YOU TRULY ARE —

ETERNAL DIVINE
LOVE CONSCIOUSNESS.

Please allow me to introduce myself —
I am *D.p.*, which stands for Divine parent. I am an icon created to help you remember who you truly are.

I was created as you were, from Divine love. I am here on a mission to remind you of the limitless power that lies within you. Your thoughts and feelings are powerful tools that will help you see why you are here on this Earth and what you are allowing yourself to experience in life.

You are an important part of the All, and everything about you impacts the cosmos. I am here to help guide you on your journey so that you can become all that you are meant to become.

PRACTICE: This week, I start to pay attention and take notice of what I think and how I feel. This daily practice will improve my ability to stay in what is called the observer state. As I listen to my words and notice my actions, I begin to identify the thoughts and habits that do not serve my best interest. I make notes on what I notice about my thoughts, feelings, and actions. I am only focused on improving my awareness this week.

It is important for me to "know thyself" for I am the one always with me no matter where I go or what challenges I face. As I work to understand my true-self and my powers, I will know how to better handle any experience I co-create.

Taking responsibility for myself is a powerful creation of manifestation. I am the only one who can truly create for me by attracting what I want from the endless possibilities offered up by the unlimited fabric of the All — Divine energy.

Every part of my life is up to me, and only me. My power lies in my thoughts, feelings, beliefs, and intentions. It is all up to me to make my life experience what I wish it to be.

PRACTICE: This week, I sit with myself daily and take note of the happenings of the day. *What did I like about my day, and what did I not like?* I make notes to help me focus on what I like. As I notice what I do not like, I rewrite the day or visualize the day with what I would have liked to experience. This should help me begin learning more about me. As I learn more about me, I can practice being the true me, and then when I know me completely, I master myself.

A Message from D.p.

I AM...

IT'S ABOUT ME.

LEARN IT!

PRACTICE IT!

MASTER IT!

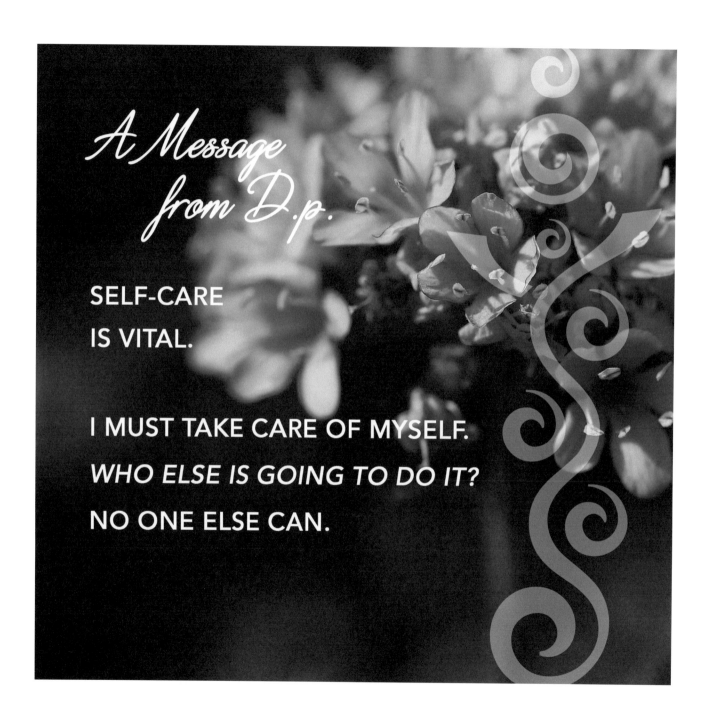

A Message from D.p.

SELF-CARE
IS VITAL.

I MUST TAKE CARE OF MYSELF.
WHO ELSE IS GOING TO DO IT?
NO ONE ELSE CAN.

If I am constantly in survival mode, I am never in creation mode. It is imperative that I take the time to address my needs and wants. When I treat myself well and embody the belief that I am worthy of self-care, I resonate out compassion and love to those around me. It's a win-win for everyone!

Despite what I may have been taught, I must now understand that it isn't just okay to put myself first — *it is vital!*

PRACTICE: This week, I take the time to really take care of my needs and wants. I embrace my true sense of worthiness and gratitude as I do this. I listen to my body, mind, and soul to know what I need to address. I give to myself first so that when I give to others and the world, I give from a place of wholeness, emanating love and light.

It is important for me to define myself because I am the only one who truly knows how I feel in any given situation. Others can only speculate. Others see my life from their perspective and through their belief systems. It is not up to me to live my life the way they expect me to; they have the Divine right to live as they wish, just as I have the Divine right to live as I wish.

PRACTICE: This week, I take notice of what I have been told I am, or should be. I ask myself if this makes me feel good. *Does it feel right to me? Or am I struggling with the limits or expectations set before me?* My life is just that — my life. It is important for me to connect with myself and keep asking questions about how I feel about what I think, say, and do. I need to be honest as I note what comes up this week.

A Reminder
from D.p.

IT ISN'T ABOUT
WHAT THEY SAY
I AM.

IT IS ABOUT
WHAT I BELIEVE
I AM.

I DEFINE MYSELF
BY WHAT
I LOVE TO BE.

Messages & Reminders

F R O M

D.p.

ABOUT MY...

Body

A Reminder from D.p.

BREATHE.

REPEAT AS NECESSARY.

Breath is life. When I breathe properly, I foster harmony within my body and exist fully in the present moment. When I am stressed or anxious, my breathing often becomes irregular. When this happens, I can return to the present moment by engaging my diaphragm and taking a few deep breaths. Many of us breathe mindlessly with our chest, but the power of conscious diaphragmatic breathing keeps us more firmly rooted in the present moment, and thus better equipped to consciously create.

PRACTICE: This week, I take note of my breathing. *Am I using my diaphragm? Is my breath keeping me rooted in the present moment?* If not, I spend a little time each day practicing deep conscious breathing.

— Notes —

What I think and feel about my body affects my body. Every thought I have is heard and heralded by each one of my cells, so when I think about how much I dislike my body, I transmit low vibrations to my cells, which creates disharmony and even disease.

Conversely, when I think about how grateful I am for my body, I transmit high vibrations to my cells, which creates harmony and good health.

It may not always seem like it, but it is a privilege to possess a physical body, for it allows me to experience the beauty of this physical dimension.

PRACTICE: This week, I pay close attention to how I think, talk, and feel about my body. My goal is to achieve a level of genuine appreciation for my body. By monitoring what I think, say, and feel, I can assess what I need to change in order to achieve a feeling of Divine love for my body.

A Message from D.p.

HOW DO I FEEL
ABOUT MY BODY?

EVERY CELL IS CONSCIOUS
AND LISTENING TO ME.

WHAT HEALS ALL?
LOVE.

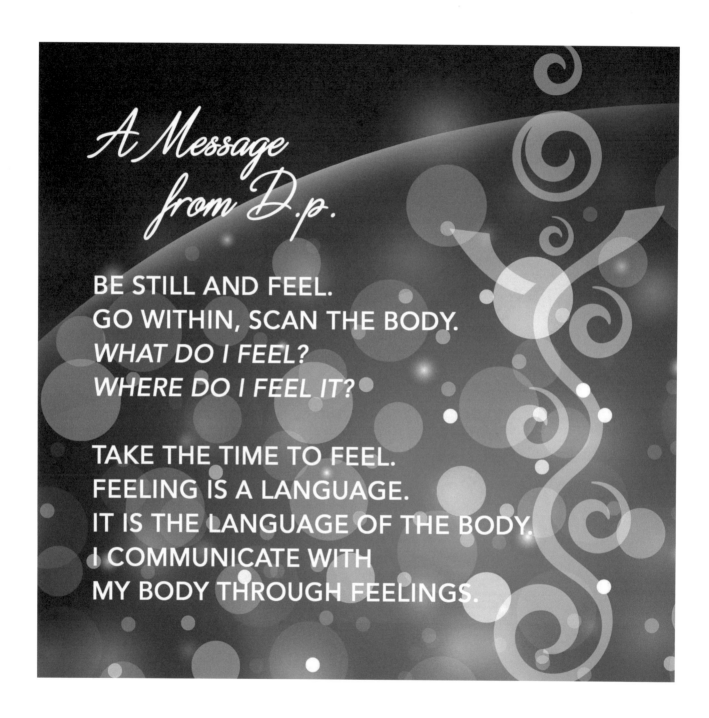

A Message from D.p.

BE STILL AND FEEL.
GO WITHIN, SCAN THE BODY.
WHAT DO I FEEL?
WHERE DO I FEEL IT?

TAKE THE TIME TO FEEL.
FEELING IS A LANGUAGE.
IT IS THE LANGUAGE OF THE BODY.
I COMMUNICATE WITH
MY BODY THROUGH FEELINGS.

My body is great at communicating to me what I feel in the present moment, for my body is always in the present moment. Based on how I feel in any given moment, I can assess whether or not I am in harmony with my true-self. If I am experiencing pain or discomfort, I know that something needs to be addressed — acknowledged, felt, released, and healed — so that I may return to harmony.

PRACTICE: This week, I work to stay aware of my bodily sensations. When I experience sensations that don't feel good, I take a moment to *focus on the sensation. What is it telling me?* If the sensation moves, I follow it. I spend as much time with it as I can until it dissipates, for I know it is trying to communicate something important. As I learn to listen to my body, I learn to listen to my true-self.

I know that when I get a scratch, my body will take care of it. It may take some time, but eventually my skin will heal. *Why, then, can my body not cure all my physical ailments?* Because I don't believe it can. It all comes back to belief. When I truly believe my body can heal itself of anything, it will.

The placebo effect proves the power of the human mind. My thoughts create my reality. The immutable laws of the universe — including the *Law of Mentalism* (All is Mind) and *Law of Attraction* (LOA) — are always working for everyone, there are no exceptions.

PRACTICE: This week, I choose to believe in the power of my body and its ability to heal itself. If I feel I need more concrete evidence, I may conduct my own research with the intention of uncovering the truth. If I am ready, I can choose to rewrite the limiting beliefs I may have about my body and embrace the healing power within.

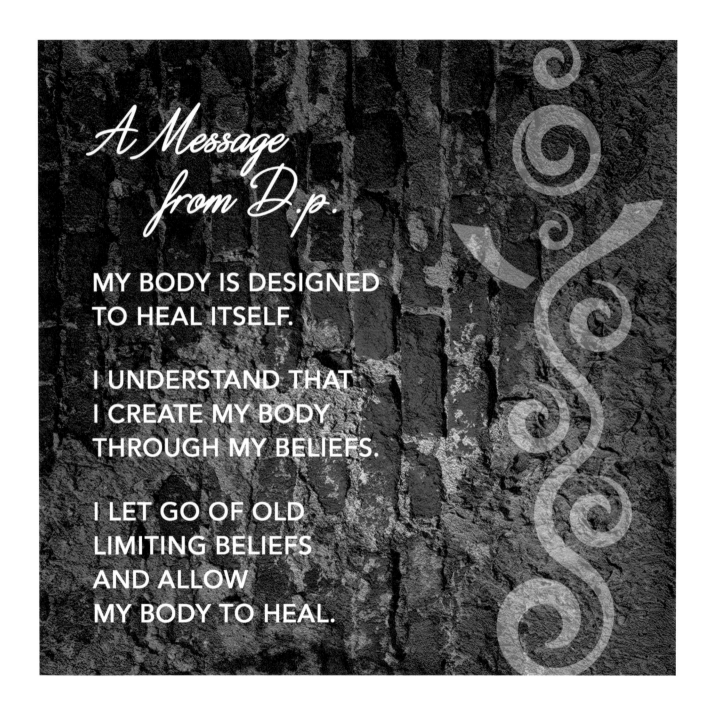

A Message from D.p.

MY BODY IS DESIGNED TO HEAL ITSELF.

I UNDERSTAND THAT I CREATE MY BODY THROUGH MY BELIEFS.

I LET GO OF OLD LIMITING BELIEFS AND ALLOW MY BODY TO HEAL.

Messages & Reminders

FROM

D.p.

ABOUT MY...

Ego

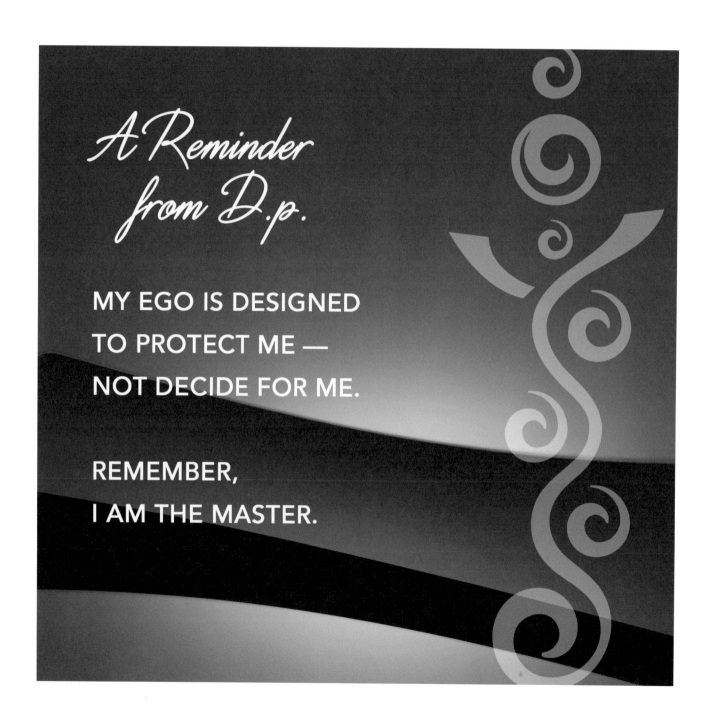

A Reminder from D.p.

MY EGO IS DESIGNED
TO PROTECT ME —
NOT DECIDE FOR ME.

REMEMBER,
I AM THE MASTER.

I know that the ego is an important element of this reality. It is designed to protect me in this dimension, and because of this, it tries to run my life. Ego energy functions through fear, and its sole mission is survival. This mentality keeps me stuck in my old programming because ego thinks that my old programs are how I'll survive; they're safe and familiar. Ego only knows my past, it does not know my future. It is constantly using data from my past experiences to detect and defend me from what it thinks are potential threats. But what ego sees as threats are not always threats, they are either illusions from my past or fear of the unknown.

If I want to evolve, I must master my ego and its fear-based programming. To do this, I must first become aware of these old programs. *What do I fear and why?* When I accept and understand my ego programs, I can then use my self-empowerment tools to rewrite them for my highest good.

PRACTICE: This week, I ask myself if I am safe to say all I need to say, do all I want to do, and follow my dreams. If I feel safe and believe that I am capable of fulfilling these desires, I set forth and do so.

If I do not feel safe or do not believe I am capable, I go inward and continue my self-work. I do this by staying aware of where I feel fear. I know these feelings come from old ego programming. I release these fears by feeling my bodily sensations (*tightness, numbness, pain, tears, hot, cold, unease, etc.*). As I do this work, I change my ego programming, expose my truth, and master my life.

Even though I am Divinely powerful, I have allowed ego to take control of my life. I do not judge myself for this, because I know it is a built-in protection mechanism. However, I am now an adult with personal power, and therefore I need to take on self-responsibility to regain control.

I remember that the ego's mission is to protect me, and that it does this by inducing fear. Fear of reliving past pain, fear of being abandoned, fear of the unknown, etc. As I become aware of ego's position in the driver's seat, I stop the car (center myself in the present moment), and respectfully order ego to move over. I take hold of the steering wheel (consciously choosing my thoughts, words, and actions) to control the journey ahead.

PRACTICE: The ego is persistent, therefore this will be a constant practice. Understand that the ego does serve a purpose: it protects me when there is danger present. But when I am trying to create the life I desire, I must quiet the ego. To do this, I pay close attention to the chatter in my mind, the fear-based programming that keeps me from evolving. I work to consciously rewrite my thoughts and rewire my thought patterns to serve my creative endeavors. I remember that I am a powerful Divine creator, and I have all that I need within me to evolve.

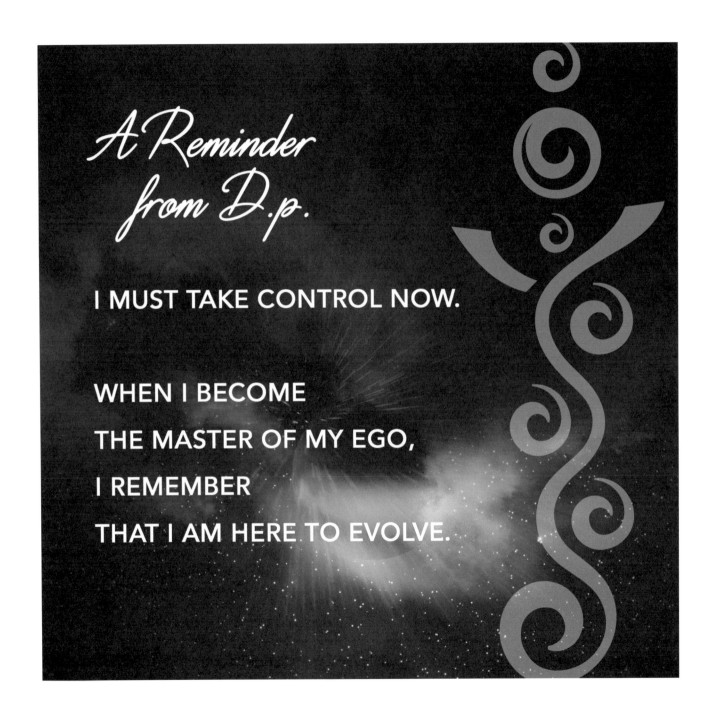

A Reminder from D.p.

I MUST TAKE CONTROL NOW.

WHEN I BECOME
THE MASTER OF MY EGO,
I REMEMBER
THAT I AM HERE TO EVOLVE.

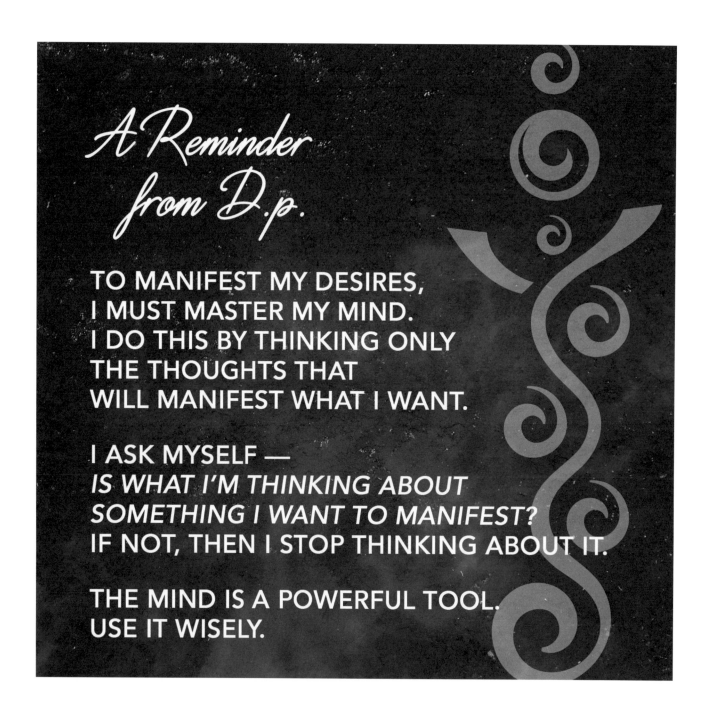

A Reminder from D.p.

TO MANIFEST MY DESIRES,
I MUST MASTER MY MIND.
I DO THIS BY THINKING ONLY
THE THOUGHTS THAT
WILL MANIFEST WHAT I WANT.

I ASK MYSELF —
*IS WHAT I'M THINKING ABOUT
SOMETHING I WANT TO MANIFEST?*
IF NOT, THEN I STOP THINKING ABOUT IT.

THE MIND IS A POWERFUL TOOL.
USE IT WISELY.

I remember that I am giving energy to what I think about and talk about, and that energy can manifest into experiences. *Am I thinking and talking about what I do not want?*

When I notice myself thinking or talking about the things I do not want to manifest, I consciously shift my focus toward that which I do want to manifest. I remember that every word has its own creative frequency, and so I must choose my words carefully.

For example: Instead of saying "I don't want to get sick," I say, "I am allowing health." The word "sick" has a frequency just like the word "health" does. I call in what I want by the words and intentions behind them.

PRACTICE: This week, I practice noticing when my negative ego-mind chatter is on autopilot. I then stop what I'm doing, take a deep breath, and redirect my focus toward something I want to create. As I do this, I notice how I feel about what I think or say. If I feel it is not true, I need to feel the sensation that comes up when I say it. This releases the negative energy related to that belief. I must stay aware of my inner-voice to ensure that the experiences I'm manifesting are the experiences I want to have. I am a powerful creator, and I know that what I focus my energy on will eventually become my reality.

— Notes —

Much like it's difficult to see the forest for the trees, it's sometimes difficult to see how good my life actually is. This is because my ego believes it must act as the conductor, directing my attention toward my survival. It is hyper-aware of potential situations that could harm me, hence the obsession with danger and drama, the addiction to fear, and the attention on lack. Ego lies to protect me and will never be satisfied, even when I get what I want.

This is why I must master my ego. I need to take control of my thoughts, and stop letting my ego influence how I see my reality. It's time to drop the veil of ego's deception and see that I am safe and have much to appreciate.

PRACTICE: This week, I take the time to look closely at my life: My relationships, my career, my living situation, my finances, my physical health, my emotional health, my self-care, etc. I ask myself how good I have it in each of these categories, making sure to be honest with myself and trying to refrain from judgment. It's okay to want something more or better, but if I am always in the *"I'll be happy when…"* state of mind, I'll never achieve true happiness or inner-peace. I must embody gratitude for all that I appreciate in my life in order to manifest more to be grateful for.

It may help me to write out exactly what I believe I want my life to look like. Then I can compare where my reality may differ and/or see how similar each area of my life actually is to the life I want to live.

A Message from D.p.

AM I LOST IN A LIE?

EGO LIES TO ME ALL THE TIME
BY TELLING ME STORIES
THAT ARE NOT TRUE.

I NEED TO LOOK MORE CLOSELY
AT MY REALITY TO SEE
IF I AM LOST IN A LIE —
MY LIFE MAY BE BETTER
THAN EGO SAYS.

Messages & Reminders

F R O M

D.p.

ABOUT MY...

Love

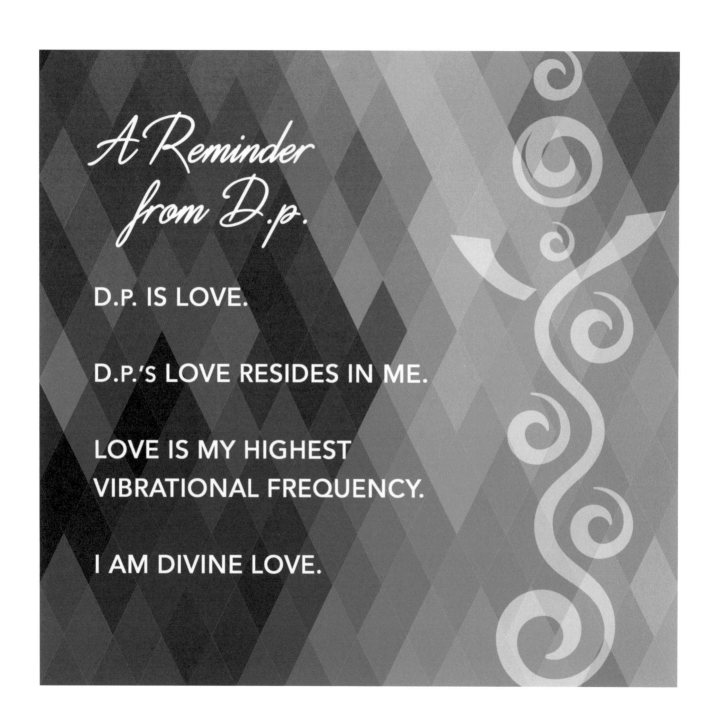

A Reminder from D.p.

D.P. IS LOVE.

D.P.'S LOVE RESIDES IN ME.

LOVE IS MY HIGHEST
VIBRATIONAL FREQUENCY.

I AM DIVINE LOVE.

D.p. is not only the icon for my Divine parent, but also for the eternal Divine love frequency that makes up the All. D.p. is part of the All, I am a part of the All, we are all eternally part of the All.

As I gain clarity on this truth, I understand that my original vibrational frequency is this Divine love frequency — the all-loving, all-accepting frequency. There is nowhere that this frequency does not exist. It is truly everywhere. It resides in all of me. It resides in every single cell of my body and in everything that makes up my cells and everything I think and feel. My entirety is made from this Divine love.

PRACTICE: For this week, I focus on implementing the belief that I am Divine love. No matter what is going on in my life, or around me, I think about and feel this truth. As I do this, I allow the Divine love vibration to resonate within and emanate from me.

D.p. represents the ideal parent and therefore does not judge what I say, do, or think. Judgment comes only from the ego, which operates using old, outdated programs that no longer serve me. It's time for an update — the D.p. version!

D.p. loves me *unconditionally*. This unconditional love accepts all of me, no matter what. There is no right or wrong, no good or bad — only love. Forever and always.

PRACTICE: This week, I focus on all I want to be, say, and do. I allow myself to become more me than I have ever been. I know that no matter what, I can express my desires and still be accepted and loved by my Divine parent. D.p. is always on my side and loves that I am me.

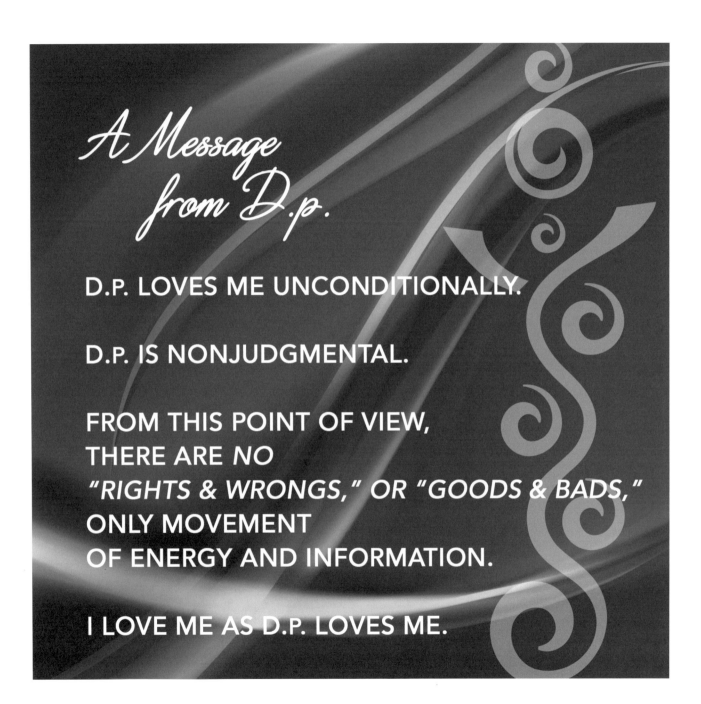

A Message from D.p.

D.P. LOVES ME UNCONDITIONALLY.

D.P. IS NONJUDGMENTAL.

FROM THIS POINT OF VIEW,
THERE ARE *NO*
"RIGHTS & WRONGS," OR "GOODS & BADS,"
ONLY MOVEMENT
OF ENERGY AND INFORMATION.

I LOVE ME AS D.P. LOVES ME.

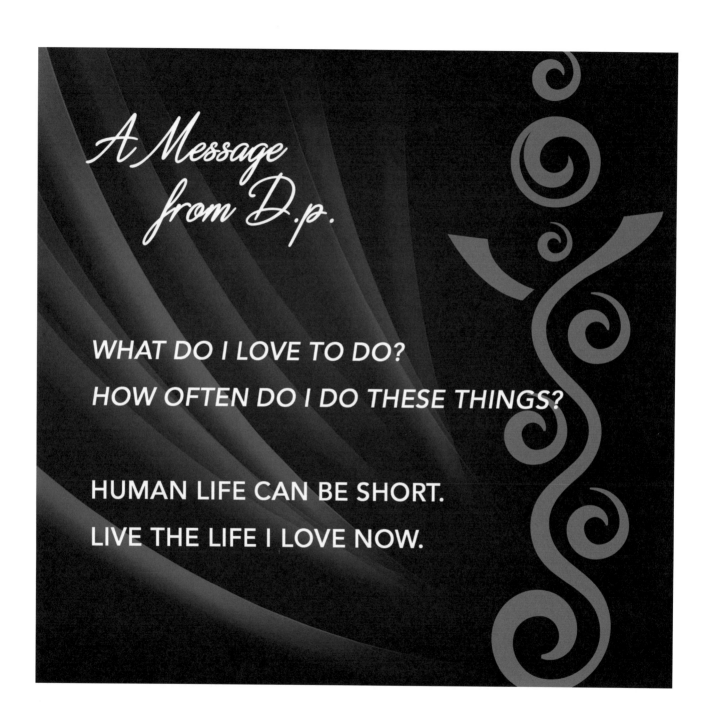

A Message from D.p.

WHAT DO I LOVE TO DO?

HOW OFTEN DO I DO THESE THINGS?

HUMAN LIFE CAN BE SHORT.

LIVE THE LIFE I LOVE NOW.

I create my life experiences, whether I know it or not. When I feel like my life is running me instead of me running my life, I must regain control. Only then can I consciously create my life the way I want it to be. Part of this process involves identifying what I love to do, what I truly love to do, and making time to do it.

What do I love to do? Take the time to think about it. It can be small things — like sitting on a park bench or walking on the beach or reading a book — or big things — like going on a trip or learning a new skill. Whatever it is, if I love it, it matters. When I allow myself to do the things I love, I become lighter, more joyous, and have more to offer myself and the world.

PRACTICE: This week, I make a list of all the things I love to do. I make sure to schedule time every day to do something I love, something that is just for me and my enjoyment. As I bring this joy into my life, I stay present and express my gratitude, thus welcoming more joy into my experience.

Everything about me began in the Divine love frequency. *Everything!* Divine love is the most powerful creative frequency there is.

I, like everyone and everything else, originated from Divine love. Because of this, I am connected to everyone and everything. All is made from Divine love.

Divine love can heal anything. It can create anything. It is the highest vibrational frequency. Once I become aware of this, once I embrace this truth, love will emanate from me, elevating not only my personal vibrational frequency, but also the collective vibrational frequency. Love can literally change the world.

PRACTICE: This week, I send love to every cell in my body. I thank them for keeping my body alive so that I may experience this life. I practice appreciating all the parts of me, even the parts I cannot see — my heart, my brain, my thoughts, my feelings, my beliefs. I recognize that they are from Divine love as well, and I allow this love to flow through me.

A Reminder from D.p.

TAKE A MOMENT
TO RAISE MY
VIBRATIONAL FREQUENCIES
TO LOVE LEVELS!

I ATTRACT WHAT I AM...

FEEL GOOD & LOVE SELF.

A Reminder from D.p.

REPEAT AFTER ME...
I LOVE MYSELF,
I LOVE MYSELF,
I LOVE MYSELF.

I MAKE THIS MY MANTRA,
AND, OF COURSE,
ONCE I BELIEVE IT, I ATTRACT LOVE —
THE HIGHEST VIBRATIONAL FREQUENCY.

Loving myself is imperative. I must love myself. If I do not make this my absolute truth, I will struggle every day until I do. Once I achieve this feeling of unconditional love for myself, my life will fall into place. When I understand that all that I want is just waiting for me to feel that I am worthy and deserving of it, I will rejoice in the ease of manifestation.

PRACTICE: Every day this week, literally say, *"I love myself."* Notice how I feel when I say this. *Is it true?* Don't let ego hide my feelings. I demand that ego let me see and feel my truth when I say these words. I get still and listen for my truth and then, as I can, I feel the sensations that will help me heal this vibrational frequency. As I work to make this belief completely true, my life will soon be flowing with ease and inner-peace.

— Notes —

Messages & Reminders

FROM

D.p.

ABOUT MY...

Fear

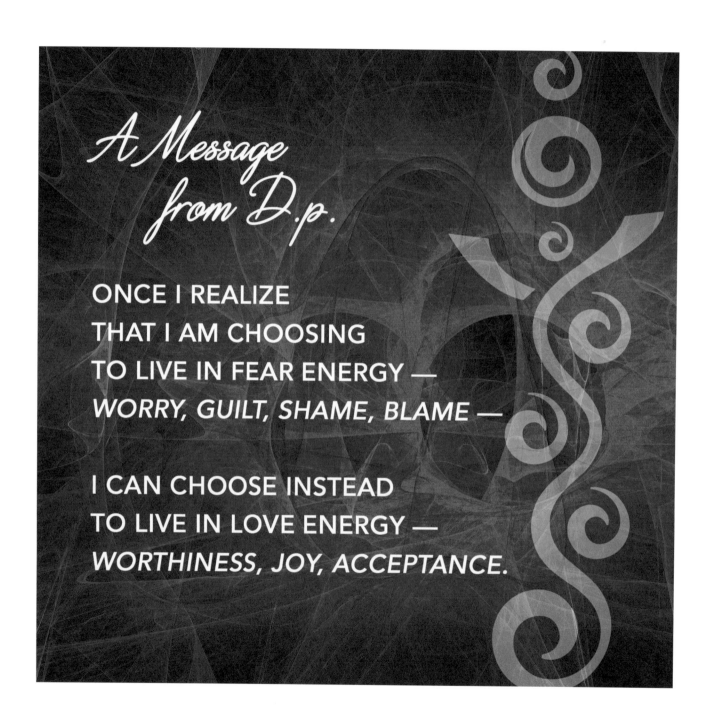

A Message from D.p.

ONCE I REALIZE
THAT I AM CHOOSING
TO LIVE IN FEAR ENERGY —
WORRY, GUILT, SHAME, BLAME —

I CAN CHOOSE INSTEAD
TO LIVE IN LOVE ENERGY —
WORTHINESS, JOY, ACCEPTANCE.

I am a powerful creator. I choose my thoughts and words and actions every moment. As I realize this, I also realize that, more often than not, I have allowed fear to run my life. These energies are expressed as worry, guilt, shame, and blame. I remember that I can choose again. I now choose thoughts of love, such as worthiness, joy, and acceptance. Only I can make this choice. It is up to me.

PRACTICE: This week, I start each day with one thought rooted in the energy of love. I remind myself throughout the day to stay in this energy no matter what is going on around me. I am powerful, and the more time I spend in the love energy, the more I positively affect the world within and around me.

— *Notes* —

Fear can be crippling — but fear isn't real, it is only a choice. Remember who I am… I am the creator, the Divine creator of my life. I am powerful beyond belief. I know this truth and use my power to believe in myself. I can create true peace within.

NOTE: Danger is real, but fear is only the projection of ego.

PRACTICE: This week, I pay attention to where I am steeped in fear-based projections and illusions. *Where are these projections coming from?* This is the time to notice if I am trapped in a fear-based illusion.

Once I recognize these fear-based illusions, I take a breath and choose to see my truth. *Am I safe? Or am I truly in danger?* Most of what I worry about never happens. I must pull myself out of the illusion of these lies.

I remember that I am in control of my life. It is up to me to see my truth and no longer play the ego game. I choose instead to focus my energy on thoughts of truth and love. It is time to look to a brighter future where I create a new, uplifting outlook that supports my evolution.

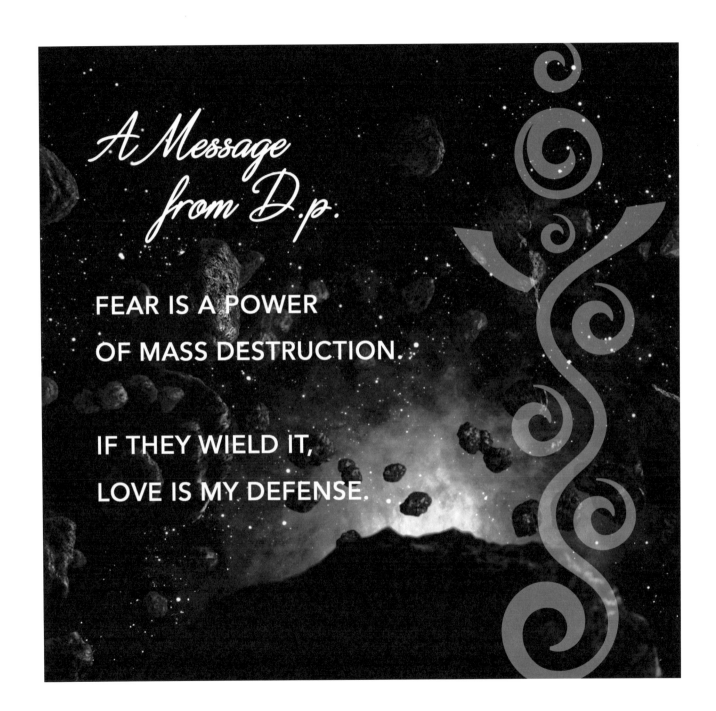

A Message from D.p.

FEAR IS A POWER
OF MASS DESTRUCTION.

IF THEY WIELD IT,
LOVE IS MY DEFENSE.

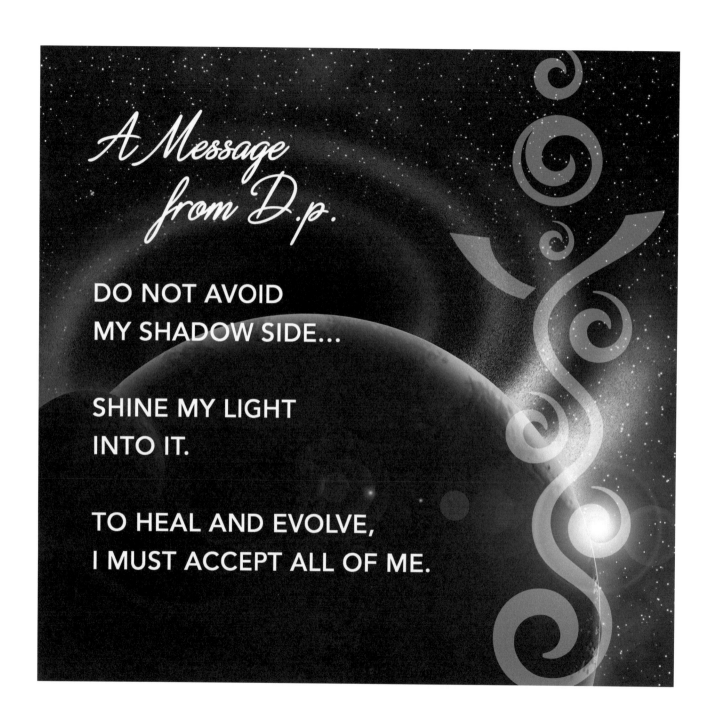

A Message from D.p.

DO NOT AVOID
MY SHADOW SIDE...

SHINE MY LIGHT
INTO IT.

TO HEAL AND EVOLVE,
I MUST ACCEPT ALL OF ME.

My shadow side is the side of me that does not embody unconditional love and acceptance. It clings to the illusion of fear-based programming that promotes victimization. This leads to feelings of separateness. This is not wrong. Nor is it right. It is just a part of me. It is all part of the journey. It serves a great purpose by showing me where I need to adjust my attitude — my frequency.

If I find myself consumed in my shadow side, attracting experiences I do not wish to have, I must recalibrate. I recognize my fears for what they are — untruths — and then send them love. The love frequency sets me free. Free to remember who I truly am — part of the Divine All.

PRACTICE: This week, when I encounter inharmonious feelings like fear and suffering, I remind myself that they are only frequencies, and that all I need to do is sit with the uncomfortable feelings until I release them. I send love to every part of me, including my shadow side.

My ego is fear-based and full of programs that are holding me back from the life I wish to live. To transcend these perceived limitations, I need to accept my truth and release the fears that hold me back from obtaining that life. I am allowed to have what I want and it is safe for me to want it.

PRACTICE: This week, I take inventory of my fears. I must be completely honest with myself. Ego consistently denies or represses my truth, so when I ask my questions, I must remember to listen with my body. *How do I feel? Am I hearing my truth?*

What in my life is not as I wish it to be? What would I like to change within my career? What would I like to change in my relationships? What would I like to change about my finances?

I remember that anything is possible if I believe it is true. But I must first recognize and release the ego fears that block or hinder my creative powers so that I can create the life I want.

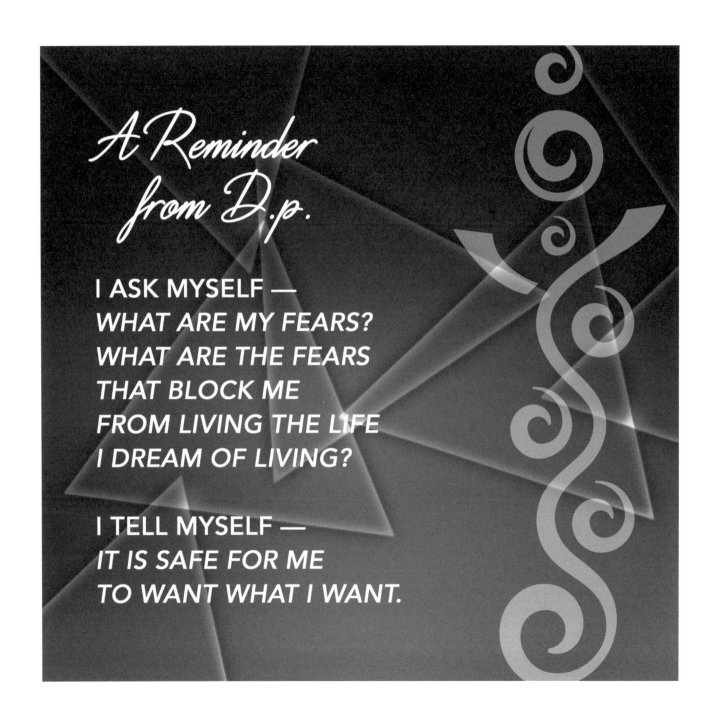

A Reminder from D.p.

I ASK MYSELF —
WHAT ARE MY FEARS?
WHAT ARE THE FEARS
THAT BLOCK ME
FROM LIVING THE LIFE
I DREAM OF LIVING?

I TELL MYSELF —
IT IS SAFE FOR ME
TO WANT WHAT I WANT.

Messages & Reminders

FROM

D.p.

ABOUT MY...

Power

A Message from D.p.

**LOA IS
LAW OF ATTRACTION...**

**LIKE VIBRATION
ATTRACTING
LIKE VIBRATION.
THIS LAW IS WORKING
ALL THE TIME!**

NEED I SAY MORE?

There are multiple Universal Laws that hold our reality together. The *Law of Attraction*, or LOA, is one of those laws. LOA is an immutable law, meaning it is at work all the time — *no exceptions!*

In essence, LOA is the principle that like vibration attracts like vibration: What I am resonating out is what I get back in return. With that in mind, I look at all that I am saying, thinking, experiencing, listening to, etc., while remembering that everything has its own unique energetic frequency vibrating out into the universe.

Because we humans are raised by other humans, we inevitably inherit many of our caregivers' beliefs, habits, outlooks, etc. As we grow into adults, we have the power to decide whether or not we want to keep what we've inherited — thus attracting more of the familiar — or forge our own path by breaking down our patterns and using LOA to manifest a new reality for ourselves.

PRACTICE: This week, I identify something in my life that I keep experiencing. *Was it an intentional manifestation or an unintentional manifestation?* If it was unintentional — meaning I did not intend to bring it into my reality — I consider how it came to be a part of my energetic resonance. If it does not serve me, I choose to use my Divine power and take the necessary steps to create something else.

Playing the victim is a common ego program that detrimentally affects my journey to self-empowerment. When I tell myself that I am at the mercy of someone or something else, I give up my conscious creative powers, and in so doing, attract similar experiences in which I feel powerless. Many of us get so lost in the victim mentality, we may not even realize what we're doing. We give all our power away to our circumstances, our past, and to the people around us, believing they dictate the limits of our reality. We are often drawn to this state of powerlessness because it comes with lessened responsibility or accountability. But therein lies the problem.

Only when I take full responsibility for my reality, for what I have co-created, can I reclaim my conscious creative powers and begin to manifest the life I desire. When I take full responsibility, I admit that it was I who attracted and allowed all those past negative experiences. And it is only I who can rewrite my reality.

PRACTICE: This week, I identify one area of my life where I feel powerless. To help me see how this victim mentality is controlling me, I take a look at my circumstances — my career, my finances, my relationships. I allow myself to see where I blame others for my suffering. Then I declare to myself that I take full responsibility for this co-creation. I understand that I attracted and allowed it into my life. Now I can examine it as a manifestation and ask myself — *why did I create it? What is my lesson?* I listen to my answer so I can learn my lesson and evolve.

A Message from D.p.

EVERY TIME
I BLAME SOMEONE ELSE
FOR MY CIRCUMSTANCES,
I AM PLAYING VICTIM.

INSTEAD, I REMEMBER THAT
I AM THE CREATOR OF MY EXPERIENCE
AND TAKE FULL RESPONSIBILITY
FOR ALL THAT I AM CREATING.
WHEN I DO THIS, I RECLAIM MY POWER.

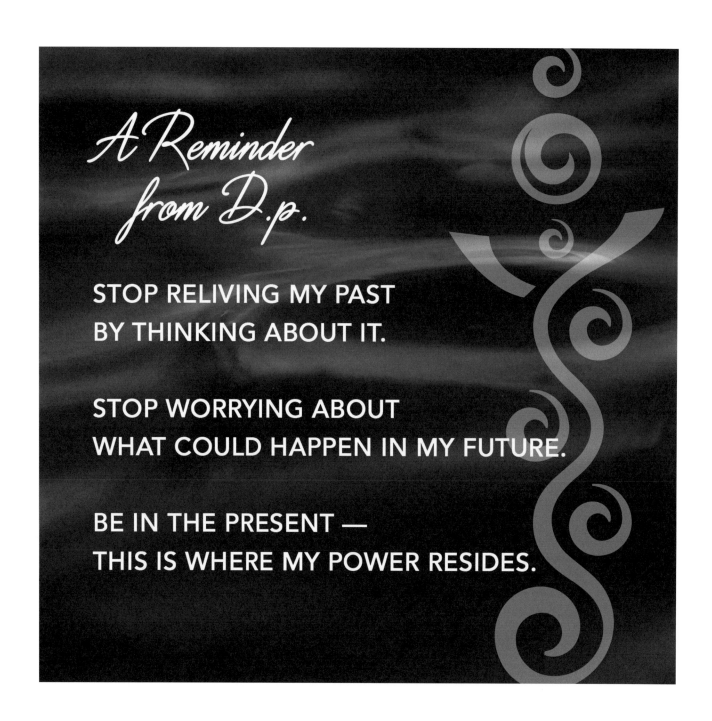

A Reminder from D.p.

STOP RELIVING MY PAST
BY THINKING ABOUT IT.

STOP WORRYING ABOUT
WHAT COULD HAPPEN IN MY FUTURE.

BE IN THE PRESENT —
THIS IS WHERE MY POWER RESIDES.

The greatest time to manifest the life I want is right now. When I live in the past, I attract more familiar experiences. When I worry about the future, I attract more things to worry about. But when I am fully in the present moment and grateful for the things I love, I attract more of what I love. When I imagine all that I desire, and live as if it is my present reality, I bring that reality to life.

PRACTICE: Notice how much energy I devote to reliving the past and fretting about the future. Then stop, take a breath, and root myself in the present moment. *What do I smell? What do I hear? What can I see? What can I feel?* Notice the here and now. Living in the present is a skill I must hone in order to create with ease.

Law of Attraction is working all the time. *Do I really want to attract the things I hate?* I know that the more I think about and talk about the things I hate, the more I will feel the feeling that I do not want to feel. This is a habit that I can rewrite. Instead of spending my energy on the things I don't like, I can choose to redirect my focus to the things I love. I am powerful and I have a choice.

PRACTICE: This week, I stay aware of the feelings in my body. When I notice that I don't feel good, I pay attention to what I am thinking about or what I am talking about. I remember that hating is a habit that I can break.

When I notice that I am in the energy of hate, I readjust my focus to the things I love to love. I make a list of all the things I love and keep it near me to help redirect my energy toward love.

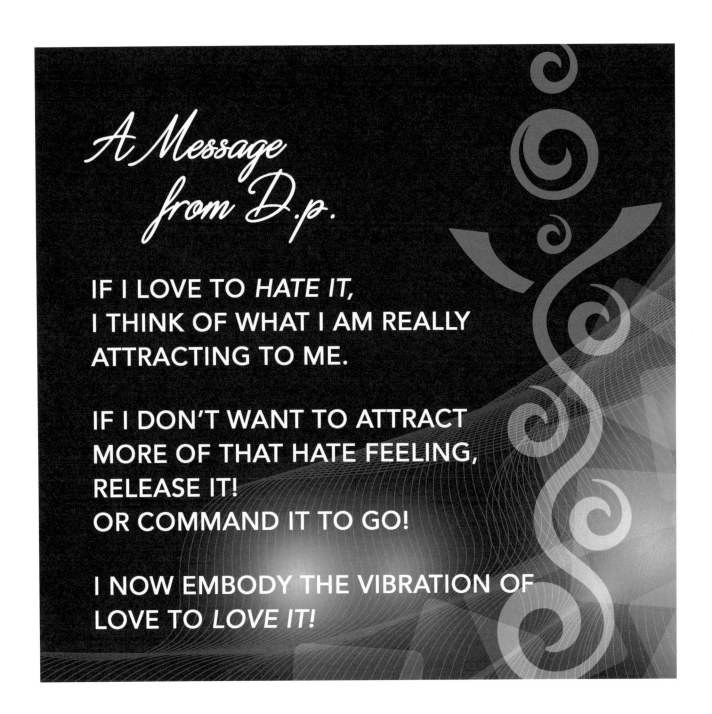

A Message from D.p.

IF I LOVE TO *HATE IT,*
I THINK OF WHAT I AM REALLY
ATTRACTING TO ME.

IF I DON'T WANT TO ATTRACT
MORE OF THAT HATE FEELING,
RELEASE IT!
OR COMMAND IT TO GO!

I NOW EMBODY THE VIBRATION OF
LOVE TO *LOVE IT!*

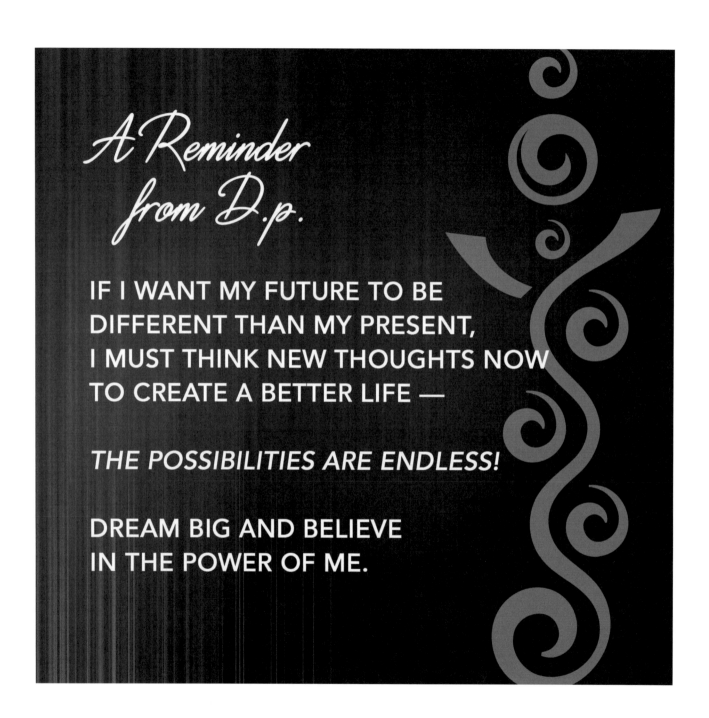

A Reminder from D.p.

IF I WANT MY FUTURE TO BE
DIFFERENT THAN MY PRESENT,
I MUST THINK NEW THOUGHTS NOW
TO CREATE A BETTER LIFE —

THE POSSIBILITIES ARE ENDLESS!

DREAM BIG AND BELIEVE
IN THE POWER OF ME.

Thoughts are powerful things. Each thought is made of energy and has a unique frequency that vibrates out into the universe. Thoughts are like magnets, attracting other thoughts with similar frequency signatures. Remember that *Law of Attraction* (LOA) is always working. Like attracts like. If I leave my mind on autopilot, letting ego run the show, I will experience an endless loop of the same thought patterns that do not serve me. But if I put in the work to master my ego-mind chatter by staying present, feeling my feelings fully, and intentionally creating what I want, my life will change for the better. I am a Divine creator, and there are no limits to what I can manifest if I truly believe it.

PRACTICE: Set my intentions to believe in my own Divine power. Remember that I am and have always been the creator of my life. It is now time for me to take control and create the reality I desire. All is possible.

— SOURCES —

Becoming Supernatural
by Dr. Joe Dizpensa

Between Death and Life
by Dolores Cannon

Biology of Belief
by Bruce Lipton, PhD

The Convoluted Universe (Books 1–5)
by Dolores Cannon

Energy Speaks
by Lee Harris

Feelings Buried Alive Never Die...
by Karol Truman

Gene Keys
by Richard Rudd

The Hidden Messages in Water
by Masaru Emoto

The Kybalion
by Three Initiates

The Life and Teachings of the Masters of the Far East
by Baird T. Spalding

Molecules of Emotion
by Candace Pert, PhD

The Power of the Subconscious Mind
by Joseph Murphy

The Secret
by Rhonda Byrne

Self-Mastery... A Journey Home to Your Self
by Hu Dalconzo

Storyblocks backgrounds

The Tao Te Ching
by Lao Tzu — translated by John Minford

The Untethered Soul
by Michael A. Singer

What the Bleep Do We Know!?
by William Arntz, Betsy Chasse, Mark Vicente

— GLOSSARY —

The All: everything that exists

Belief: a conscious or subconscious program that creates the reality of my life experience

Conscious Mind: my awareness

Divine (All/Creator/Source): true/eternal all-loving, all-accepting love frequency

D.p.: Divine parent — icon representing eternal all-loving, all-accepting self

Ego (Ego-mind): the subconscious/ unconscious programming to protect self

Energy: the fabric of the universe used for creation of matter and non-matter

Fear: an illusion created by the ego

Feeling: a sensation in the body

First Person: thinking and speaking in "me, my," and "I" language so as to create permanent behavioral change by accepting complete responsibility

Free Will: the Divine right of choice that all humans possess

Integrity: being honorable and true

Intention: a thought with feeling that is set forth to create a desired outcome

Law Of Attraction (LOA): a universal law that states like vibration attracts like vibration

Law Of Mentalism: a universal law that states All is mind. An immutable law of the universe

Love: eternal, unconditional, all-accepting

Mantra: a repeated sound or phrase while in a meditative state

Power: control, command, dominion, sovereignty

Sensation: a feeling in the body such as pain, tightness, heaviness, heat, tears, numbness, nausea, etc.

True-self: eternal Divine being that knows the truth and purpose of one's experience

Truth: where one's self-harmony resides

— ABOUT THE AUTHOR —

Dr. Sherrilyn Kirchner (Dr. K.) is a metaphysician and owner/founder of Holistic Life Source. Dr. K. works as an online life coach, holistic counselor, and meditation instructor. She offers a self-mastery video series, a D.p. video series, and other enlightening materials on her website: www. holisticlifesource.com.

Dr. K. lives in Indiana with her husband and two children. She dedicates her time to teaching self-mastery techniques through multiple formats to best help her clients holistically evolve into their truest selves.

— ACKNOWLEDGMENTS —

I would like to thank my family, friends, and teachers for the amazing support they gave me as I embarked on this journey. While my kids were the original motive for my desire to create a better life, I quickly saw the power of this material, and wanted to share the empowering benefits with others. This is how it became my profession. It has been a challenging endeavor, but well worth every effort. My life experience has benefited greatly from the implementation of this powerful knowledge.

I would like to express my gratitude to my husband and children, who encouraged me to pursue this passion. I would like to especially thank my daughter, Kasey, who helped edit this book and many other Holistic Life Source productions.

— *Notes* —

— *Notes* —

— *Notes* —

Printed in the United States
by Baker & Taylor Publisher Services